CHIKYU MISAKI

Chapter 1:
The Snow-colored Boy

Table of Contents

5

FROM NOW ON, THIS IS YOUR NEW HOME, MISAKI-CHAN.

KACHAK

YOU CAME HERE ONCE A LONG TIME AGO.

BUT I WAS ONLY ABOUT FOUR YEARS OLD THEN. I DON'T REMEMBER IT MUCH.

Hmm...

SURE IS AN OLD BUILDING.

6

STILL...

THE WHOLE HOUSE WAS FULL OF THOSE THINGS.

WHERE ARE THEY NOW?

PROFESSOR OTORI HAD A COLLECTION OF ANIMAL, PLANT AND DINOSAUR FOSSILS. HE WAS RESEARCHING EVOLUTION.

SEEMS LIKE THERE WAS A WHOLE LOT MORE STUFF IN HERE THEN.

YOU MEAN THE FOSSIL SPECIMENS.

TAX ON THE HOUSE?

Hmph!

THAT'S NOT FAIR.

PROFESSOR OTORI MADE A DEAL WITH THE MUSEUM OVER IN *MISAKI* CITY.

IN EXCHANGE FOR HIS COLLECTION, THE MUSEUM WOULD PAY OFF YOUR INHERITANCE TAX ON THE HOUSE.

THEY WEREN'T THE KIND OF THINGS YOU COULD TAKE CARE OF WITHOUT SPECIAL TRAINING.

AND YOU GET TO KEEP THE PROPERTY.

WELL, I THINK YOU GOT A GOOD DEAL.

OF COURSE NOT! NOBODY WANTS TO PAY TAXES!

Ha Ha Ha

YOU HAVE TO PAY NATIONAL HEALTH INSURANCE, TOO.

YOU DON'T HAVE TO PUT IT LIKE *THAT*.

OH?

ha... ha haha...

SPEAKING OF WHICH, THIS HOUSE AND LAND ALL BELONG TO *YOU*, MISAKI.

WINK

LEGALLY, *KYOICHI* IS MERELY A GUEST IN YOUR HOME.

8

WHAT DO YOU MEAN?

ACCORDING TO THE WILL, ALL THE PROPERTY GOES TO THE SURVIVING BLOOD RELATIVE.

WE'RE THE SAME FAMILY, AREN'T WE?

PROFESSOR OTORI WAS YOUR MOTHER'S GRANDFATHER.

KYOICHI-SAN DOESN'T GET A DIME.

SNICKER SNICKER

WELL, I GUESS YOU COULD!

H-HEY... MISAKI!

SO IF I GET SICK OF HIM, I CAN THROW HIM OUT?

REALLY?

UH... YEAH... H-HA HA...

SNICKER

SNICKER

HMMM

HMPH!

BUT IF THAT HAPPENS, YOU CAN COME STAY WITH ME!

11

DAD...
WHAT
A JERK!

THIS
MUST
HAVE
BEEN
MOM'S
ROOM
WHEN
SHE
WAS
LITTLE.

12

16

YAAAWN.

CHIRP CHIRP

CHIRP CHIRP

I FEEL LIKE I HAD SOME REALLY STRANGE DREAM.

creak

creak

DAD? ARE YOU...

DAD?

creak

CRASH

SO...

...*THAT'S* WHY YOU MOVED HERE.

DAD DOESN'T REALLY LIKE NOISY CITIES ANYWAY.

WITH THE INTERNET, HE CAN WORK FROM ANYWHERE.

YUP!

HEH!

IT'S LIKE ANNE SHIRLEY IN "ANNE OF GREEN GABLES."

NAH, IT'S NATURAL.

WHO'S ANNE SHIRLEY?

I *WISH* THAT WAS TRUE.

SOUNDS LIKE A COOL DAD.

IS YOUR HAIR DYED?

IT'S SUCH A BEAUTIFUL DEEP RED.

PEEP

20

23

28

PAH

AHH

LET'S TAKE HIM HOME!

HE REALLY SEEMS TO *LIKE* YOU, MISAKI-CHAN!

AND THIS WAY, HE LOOKS JUST LIKE A REGULAR BOY.

HUH?! BUT...

I'VE *NEVER* SEEN AN ANIMAL THIS *CUTE!*

RIGHT?

SEE?

SEE?

SEE? HE *WANTS* TO BE WITH YOU.

ROLL

ROLL

LOOK!

SNUGGLE SNUGGLE

HE CAN WEAR MY LITTLE BROTHER'S OLD CLOTHES.

HOLD ON! WAIT A MINUTE!

C'MON! LET'S *DO* IT!

40

41

45

46

48

49

NEO! COME BACK HERE!

HUH?!

TAKE OFF THOSE WET PANTS!

WHUMP

WHUMP

OKAY.

I'LL BE WORKING IN MY ROOM.

WHUMP

WHUMP

LATER!

SAY, MISAKI... ABOUT THIS KID...I...

52

53

58

60

61

64

IT WAS LIKE SHE JUST CALLED HIM THAT ON THE SPOT.

UH...

WE WERE PLAYING THE VIDEO THAT DAY, REMEMBER?

NEO IS THE NAME OF THE MAIN CHARACTER IN "THE MATRIX."

WHAT, DIDN'T YOU NOTICE?

JUST BECAUSE NOBODY HAS REPORTED HIM MISSING, IT DOESN'T MEAN NOBODY'S LOOKING FOR HIM.

LET'S JUST... SEE WHAT HAPPENS.

HOLD ON A SECOND.

THEN I GUESS WE BETTER CALL THE POLICE.

TOTTER TOTTER

Sniff Sniff

sniff

PEPO

WELL, IF YOU SAY SO.

SLIP

SNAP

?

POLICE ARE TRYING TO CONFIRM THE SAFETY OF THE CHILD.

KIDNAPPERS OF THE GRAND-DAUGHTER OF THE CHAIRMAN OF THE ASAI CORPORATION HAVE DEMANDED A RANSOM OF 240 MILLION YEN.

I THINK THAT WOULD BE BEST, FOR NOW.

SOMY

TOP TONIGHT'S AND STORY.

?

LET'S GET THE GUY BIG SIS TALKED ABOUT YESTERDAY. THE FOREIGN GUY.

YEAH!

YOU GOIN' OUT LOOKIN' FOR MONSTERS?

IF YOU'RE *GONNA* HUNT MONSTERS, FIRST YOU *GOTTA* GATHER A TEAM.

SHUMP

SHUMP

SHUMP

HEY, *WAIT!*

SHHH

TA TA TA

THE CORD GOT PULLED OUT.

HOW'D THAT HAP-PEN?

KNOCK KN

?

70

MY GREAT GRAND-FATHER?

SOME GUY NAMED PROFESSOR OTORI FOUND IT.

BUT THE ONLY REAL BONES WERE THE PELVIS AND THE RIBS. THE REST WERE RECON-STRUCTIONS.

I SAW IT ONCE.

THAT'S A PTERO-DACTYL FOSSIL IN THE MISAKI CITY MUSEUM.

MY GREAT GRANDFATHER...

HEY!

WHAT HAPPENED TO NEO?

?

76

83

2 END

Chapter 3:
The Bad Girl

93

96

100

101

JUST IN. THIS

ASAI TOKUKO, KIDNAPPED HEIRESS OF THE ASAI CONGLOMERATE, HAS BEEN RELEASED UNHARMED.

"TWO HOSTAGES," EH?

HOWEVER, THE KIDNAPPERS APPEAR TO HAVE ESCAPED WITH THE RANSOM.

IT IS STILL NOT CLEAR WHETHER THE OTHER HOSTAGE, TOKUKO'S PRIVATE TUTOR, FUJIKAWA REIKO, HAS BEEN RELEASED.

STAND

MINUTES AGO, THE PO-LICE--

CLICK

ROUGH WEATHER TODAY.

CREAK

DRAG DRAG

MISAKI-CHAN.

AH...

WHAT ARE YOU STARING AT?

LOOK. I SAW THE NEWS ON MY CELL PHONE.

REALLY?

HEY, DID YOU HEAR?

THAT GIRL WHO GOT KIDNAPPED WAS RELEASED.

240 MILLION...

ISN'T SHE THE SAME AGE AS US?

108

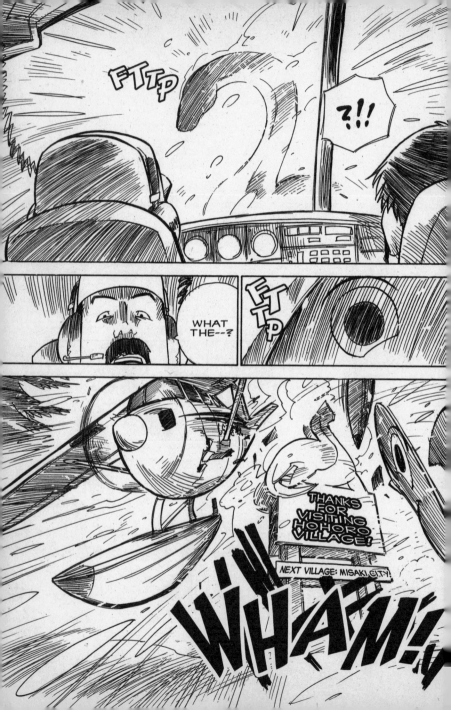

114

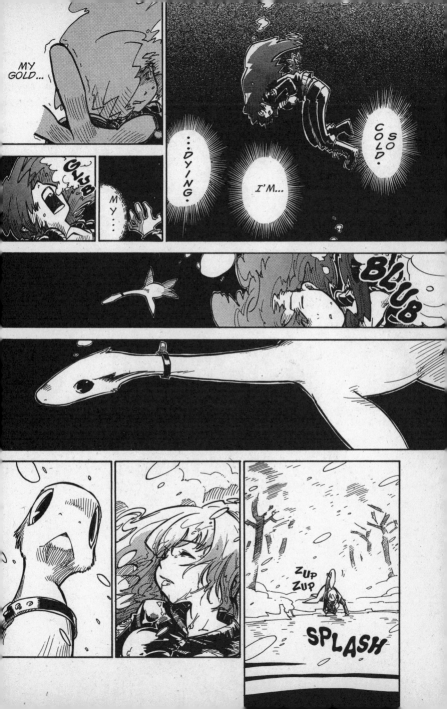

122

Chapter 4:
The Welcoming Party

124

125

126

127

128

YOU PEOPLE ARE DEPRESS-ING.

KACHAK

PRETTY TOUGH FOR A FOURTEEN-YEAR-OLD GIRL WHO WAS STILL A HOSTAGE THIS MORNING.

SHE WAS ELITE FROM THE DAY SHE WAS BORN.

SLAM

133

SHUUP

FWAP!

THE PERSON WHO KNOWS MY SECRET.

FUJIKAWA REIKO.

...I NEVER SHOULD HAVE SHOWN HER MY WEAKNESS.

IT DOESN'T MATTER HOW CONFINED WE WERE...

THE ONLY ONE WHO SHOULD KNOW THAT SECRET...

squeak

squeak

squeak

squeak

143

144

148

SLAM

WHAT'S UP WITH HIM?

MAYBE THAT'S THE GUY WE WERE SUPPOSED TO MEET AT THE LAKE!

ANYWAY...

I BETTER DRESS AND GET SOMETHING TO EAT.

CLATTER

IT'S POSSIBLE.

NOBODY IN THE OPERATION KNOWS ANYBODY ELSE!

SO THEN HE WOULDN'T KNOW ME.

152

WHAT KIND OF PERSON WAS YOUR MOTHER?

WELL...

SHE'S *KINDA* LIKE AOI-SAN.

SHE'S THE SIMPLE TYPE. SAYS EXACTLY WHAT SHE'S THINKING.

BUT THREE YEARS AGO SHE GOT STUNG BY A BEE AND DIED.

AND THEY WERE EVEN FRIENDS.

I GUESS THAT'S WHAT BUGS ME.

SOUNDS CRAZY, DOESN'T IT?

THE DOCTOR SAID IT SET OFF A MASSIVE ALLERGIC REACTION.

A BEE?

I COULDN'T BELIEVE IT.

154

4 END

Chapter 5:
A Mysterious Alliance

162

169

170

173

175

176

177

178

181

CHIRP

CHIRP

YAWN!

u/p

THAT'S NOT FAIR. YOU MAKE OTHER PEOPLE SLEEP ALONE.

Heh heh heh

WE GOT SO BUSY SNUGGLING, WE COULDN'T CLOSE OUR EYES.

WE DIDN'T GET A WINK OF SLEEP.

MORNING!

WHAT'S WRONG?

DING DONG

WILL YOU QUIT TALKING ABOUT HIM LIKE THAT, PLEASE?

YES.

STILL, I CAN'T GET OVER HOW HUMAN HE LOOKS.

SAY, WHO'S THIS KID?

UH... ER...

HE'S THE CHILD OF A FOREIGN FRIEND, COME TO VISIT.

WELL, WELL. HE SAID HE WANTED TO SEE SNOW.

WE'RE GOING TO START EXAMINING THE PLANE AND BREAKING IT DOWN. I HOPE WE DON'T CAUSE YOU TOO MUCH INCONVENIENCE.

WELL, THANKS FOR THE NOTICE.

MORNING.

OH...

GOOD MORNING, SIR.

KACHAK

ARE THEY GONNA PUT US ON T.V.?

HUH?

BY THE WAY...

SOME OF THE NEWS MEDIA MIGHT START SHOWING UP, SO YOU BETTER WATCH OUT FOR THEM.

THAT'S IT?

IT'S A MINOR STORY.

YEAH, MAYBE A LITTLE BIT.

HA HA HA

東製材所

183

WHAT'S THAT FOR?

LOOK AT THE SIZE!

WOW

HERE WE HAVE A FRESH TUNA.

SOMY

KHH.. KK KESHAK

DO YOU HAVE ANYTHING TO EAT HERE?

. . . .

ARE YOU GOING HUNT- ING?

OR MAYBE YOU'RE PLANNING ON SHOOTING SOMEBODY?

I KILLED A DEER YESTERDAY. THE MILK AND BUTTER I GOT FROM THE OKOUCHI FARM DOWN THE ROAD.

IT TASTES OKAY.

BLOP BLOP BLOP

KESHAK

UMM.

NOT TOO BAD.

slurp

IF YOU DON'T HANDLE A BABY LIKE THIS EVERY DAY...

IT WON'T PERFORM WHEN THE TIME COMES THAT YOU NEED IT.

!

DO YOU KNOW ANYTHING ABOUT THE CESSNA THAT CRASHED YESTER- DAY?

CHIK
CHIK

A CESSNA?

IT'S ON THE NEWS. LOOK.

NEARBY HERE.

SO IT *DID* CRASH...

THE PILOT, TAJIMURA MITSUHIRO, DIED ON IMPACT.

...A PASSENGER WAS TAKEN TO MISAKI CITY HOSPITAL, AND IS LISTED IN CRITICAL CONDITION. HIS IDENTITY HAS NOT YET BEEN ESTABLISHED.

...THAT A SMALL CESSNA CRASHED AFTER COLLIDING WITH THE HOHORO VILLAGE WELCOME SIGN.

CHIK

...THAT *HARD-HEADED* THUG DIDN'T DIE!

DAMN!

!

186

188

TWO PEOPLE HAVE AN AFFAIR.

EVEN RUMORS SMALL AS THAT SPREAD FAST IN A SMALL TOWN LIKE THIS.

......

IT'S LIKE I SAID BEFORE.

THIS IS A SMALL TOWN.

......

OUTSIDE OF THE TOURIST SEASON, IT'S STRANGE FOR ANY OUTSIDER TO COME HERE.

IT WILL TAKE TIME TO PULL ALL THAT GOLD FROM THE BOTTOM OF THE LAKE.

MAYBE THERE IS SOME VALUE TO STAYING HERE.

AND I'VE GOT TO STAY OUT OF SIGHT.

SO WHAT IS IT YOU WANT FROM ME?

YOU'LL SEE SOON.

OKAY, YOU'VE GOT A DEAL.

AND THE BOY WITH THE COLLAR IS SOMEWHERE AROUND HERE, TOO.

YOU MEAN YOU'LL SHOW ME TONIGHT, RIGHT?

FINE.

YOU DON'T ASK ANYTHING ABOUT ME.

BUT I HAVE A CONDITION OF MY OWN.

cmx

...KYU MISAKI vol. 1 © 2001 Yuji Iwahara. First
...ished in Japan in 2001 by Kadokawa Shoten
...lishing Co., Ltd., Tokyo.

...KYU MISAKI vol. 1, published by WildStorm
...oductions, an imprint of DC Comics, 888 Prospect
... #240, La Jolla, CA 92037. English Translation ©
...05. All Rights Reserved. English translation rights
...ranged with Kadokawa Shoten Publishing Co., Ltd.,
...okyo, through Tuttle-Mori Agency, Inc., Tokyo. The
...tories, characters, and incidents mentioned in this
...magazine are entirely fictional. Printed on recyclable
...paper. WildStorm does not read or accept unsolicited
...submissions of ideas, stories or artwork. Printed in
...Canada.

DC Comics, a Warner Bros.
Entertainment Company.

Translation and adaptation – Jonathan Tarbox

Janice Chiang – Lettering

John J. Hill – CMX Logo & publication design

Larry Berry/Ed Roeder – Additional Design

Ben Abernathy – Editor

ISBN: 1-4012-0799-5

Jim Lee
    Editorial Director
John Nee
    VP—Business Development
Hank Kanalz
    VP—General Manager, WildStorm
Paul Levitz
    President & Publisher
Georg Brewer
    VP—Design & DC Direct Creative
Richard Bruning
    Senior VP—Creative Director
Patrick Caldon
    Senior VP—Finance & Operations
Chris Caramalis
    VP—Finance
Terri Cunningham
    VP—Managing Editor
Stephanie Fierman
    Senior VP—Sales & Marketing
Alison Gill
    VP—Manufacturing
Rich Johnson
    VP—Book Trade Sales
Lillian Laserson
    Senior VP & General Counsel
Paula Lowitt
    Senior VP—Business & Legal Affairs
David McKillips
    VP—Advertising & Custom Publishing
Gregory Noveck
    Senior VP—Creative Affairs
Cheryl Rubin
    Senior VP—Brand Management
Jeff Trojan
    VP—Business Development, DC Direct
Bob Wayne
    VP—Sales